HOUGHTON MIFFLIN HARCOU

FLORIDA
JOURNEYS

Program Authors

James F. Baumann · David J. Chard · Jamal Cooks · J. David Cooper · Russell Gersten · Marjorie Lipson
Lesley Mandel Morrow · John J. Pikulski · Héctor H. Rivera · Mabel Rivera · Shane Templeton · Sheila W. Valencia
Catherine Valentino · MaryEllen Vogt

Consulting Author

Irene Fountas

Cover illustration by Scott Nash.

Printed in the U.S.A.

ISBN 978-0-547-86675-8

7 8 9 10   0868   21 2 0 19 18 17 16 15 14

4500477397   C D E F G

HOUGHTON MIFFLIN HARCOURT

Unit 1

2

3

Unit 2

Unit 3

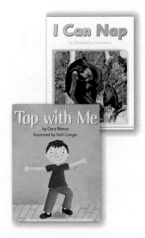

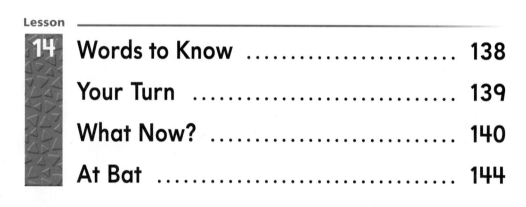

7

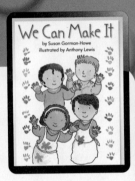

☑ **WORDS TO KNOW**
High-Frequency Words

I

Vocabulary Reader

Context Cards

K.RI.1.1 ask and answer questions about key details; **K.RF.3.3.c** read common high-frequency words by sight; **K.SL.1.2** confirm understanding of a text read aloud or information presented orally or through other media by asking/answering questions and requesting clarification

Words to Know

Read Together

▸ Read the word.

▸ Talk about the picture.

I

I have a big family!

Your Turn

Talk About It!

What Makes a Family?
by Pam Muñoz Ryan

Families are different. What is the same about all families? Share ideas with a partner.

See What We Can Do

by Susan Gorman-Howe

illustrated by Sue Dennen

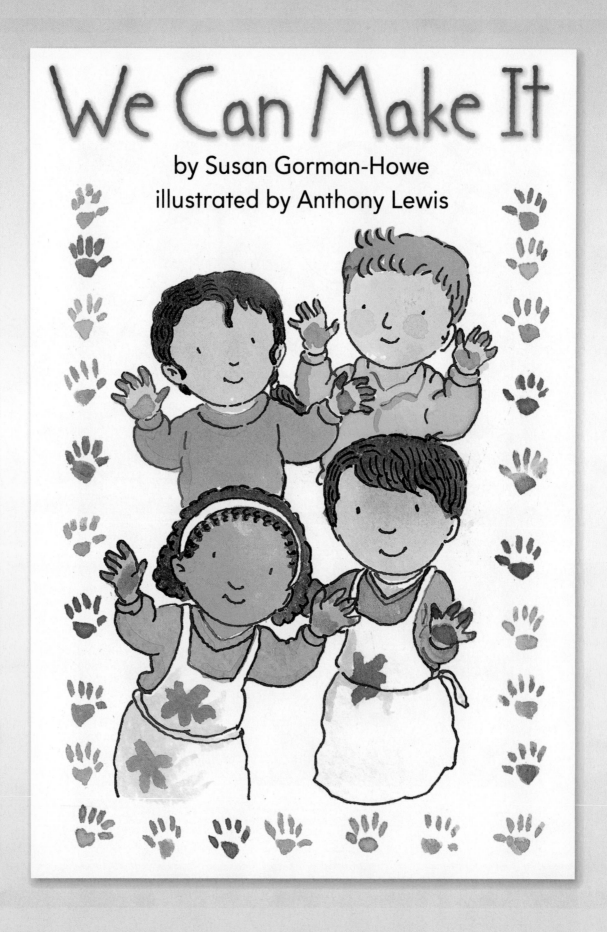

We Can Make It

by Susan Gorman-Howe

illustrated by Anthony Lewis

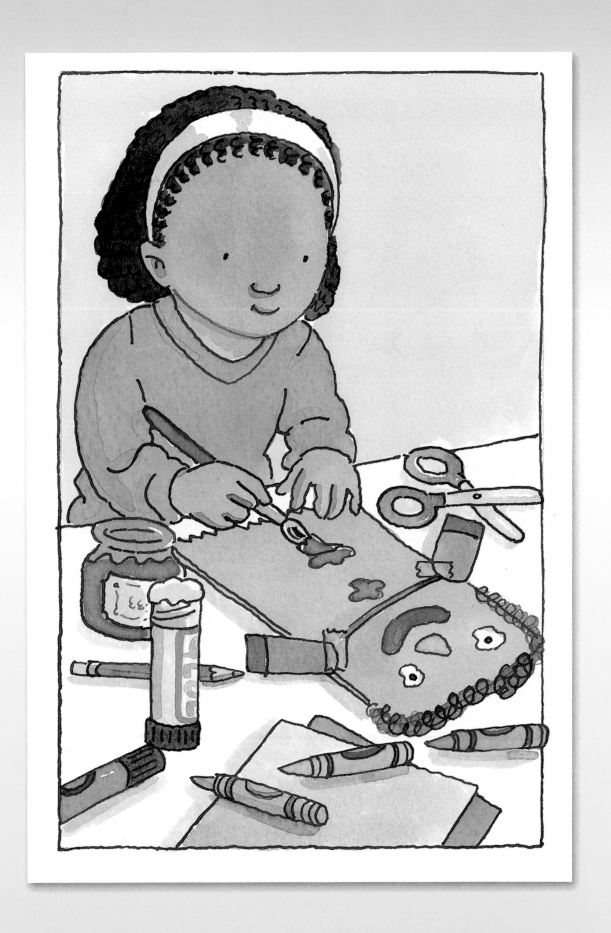

Words to Know

Read Together

We Go to School
by Susan Gorman-Howe
illustrated by Maryann Cocca-Leffler

I Like
by Owen Marcus
illustrated by Maribel Suarez

✓ WORDS TO KNOW
High-Frequency Words

like

Vocabulary Reader

At School
by Philip Rush

Context Cards

K.RL.1.1 Ask and answer questions about key details; **K.RF.3.3.c** Read common high-frequency words by sight; **K.SL.1.2** confirm understanding of a text read aloud or information presented orally or through other media by asking/ answering questions and requesting clarification

Go Digital

- ▶ Read the word.
- ▶ Talk about the picture.

like

We like to go to school!

18

Your Turn

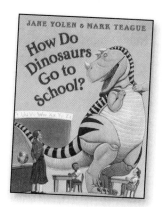

Talk About It!

Why do we have rules at school? Talk about it with a friend.

We Go to School

by Susan Gorman-Howe

illustrated by Maryann Cocca-Leffler

I Like

by Owen Marcus

illustrated by Maribel Suarez

I like  .

I like .

I like .

I like .

✓ **WORDS TO KNOW**
High-Frequency Words

the

Vocabulary Reader

Context Cards

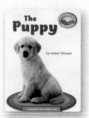

K.RL.1.3 identify characters, settings, and major events; **K.RF.3.3.c** read common high-frequency words by sight

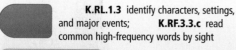

Go Digital

Words to Know

Read Together

▸ Read the word.

▸ Talk about the picture.

the

1

Do you see the puppy?

Your Turn

Talk About It!

Talk to a friend. Tell why pets need someone to take care of them.

Baby Bear's Family

by Susan Gorman-Howe

illustrated by Angela Jarecki

I like the .

The Party

by Ron Kingsley

illustrated by Yvette Banek

I like the .

I like the .

34

36

I like the .

and

**Vocabulary
Reader**

**Context
Cards**

K.RI.1.3 describe the connection between individuals, events, ideas, or information in a text; **K.RF.3.3.c** read common high-frequency words by sight

Words to Know

Read Together

▸ Read the word.

▸ Talk about the picture.

and

A worker has a saw and a hammer.

38

Your Turn

Talk About It!

What kinds of work do people do? Tell a partner.

Mm

by Pat Macnan

illustrated by
Diana Schoenbrun

Mm

Mm

I Like Mm

by Pat Macnan

I like the .

I like the .

I like the .

Mm

I like the ☐ and the ❀❀.

Ss
by Pat Macnan
illustrated by Diana Schoenbrun

I Like Ss
by Pablo Lopez

✓ WORDS TO KNOW
High-Frequency Words

I

like

Vocabulary Reader

Make a Kite
By Becca Houston
HOUGHTON MIFFLIN

Context Cards

I have a big family!

K.RI.3.7 describe relationships between illustrations and the text;
K.RF.3.3.c read common high-frequency words by sight

Go Digital

48

Words to Know

Read Together

▸ You learned these words. Use each one in a sentence.

I

I have a big family!

like

We like to go to school!

Your Turn

Talk About It!

The Handiest Things
in the World
ANDREW CLEMENTS
Photographs by Raquel Jaramillo

How do tools help us do
things with our hands?
Tell a partner what you think.

Ss

by Pat Macnan

illustrated by Diana Schoenbrun

51

I Like Ss

by Pablo Lopez

I like the .

Ss

I like the .

I like the ☀.

Ss

I like the 🫗 and the 🥪.

Aa
by Roberto Livingston
illustrated by Bernard Adnet

I See
by Sheila Hoffman

✓ WORDS TO KNOW
High-Frequency Words

see

Vocabulary Reader

Look at Me!
by Olivia Rose
Illustrated by Marilyn Jesmotta

Context Cards

What can you see in the city?

K.RI.1.1 ask and answer questions about key details; **K.RF.3.3.c** read common high-frequency words by sight

Go Digital

Words to Know
Read Together

▸ Read the word.

▸ Talk about the picture.

see

What can you see in the city?

Your Turn

Talk About It!

How do you use your senses to learn about the world? Tell a friend.

Aa

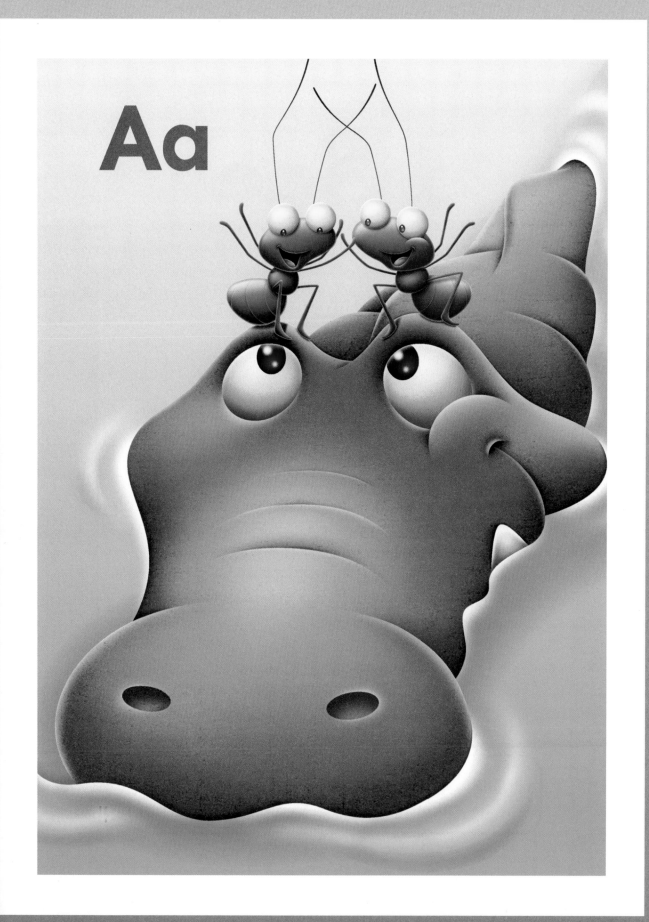

I See

by Sheila Hoffman

I see the .

Aa

I see the .

Aa

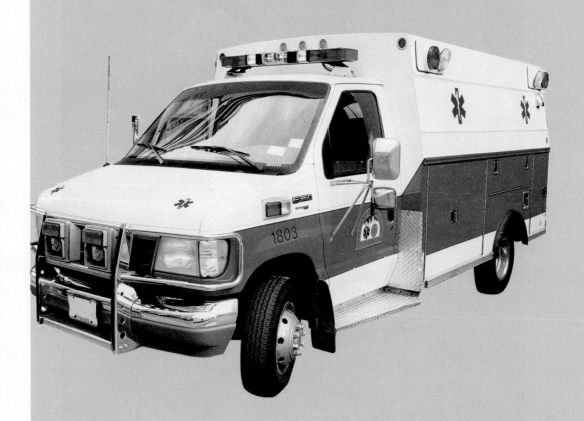

I see the .

Aa

I see the .

Tt
by Nimesh Sing
illustrated by Priscilla Burris

We Like Toys
by Matthew Lorer

☑ WORDS TO KNOW
High-Frequency Words

we

Vocabulary Reader

On the Farm
by Alex Corro

Context Cards

Our cat purrs when we pet her.

K.RL.1.1 ask and answer questions about key details; **K.RF.3.3.c** read common high-frequency words by sight

Go Digital

68

Words Read Together to Know

▸ Read the word.

▸ Talk about the picture.

we

Our cat purrs when **we** pet her.

Your Turn

Talk About It!

How do people and animals communicate? Talk about it with a friend. Use words from the **Big Book** as you share ideas.

Tt

by Nimesh Sing

illustrated by Priscilla Burris

Tt

72

Tt

We Like Toys

by Matthew Lorer

Tt

I like the .

Tt

We like the 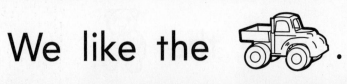.

Tt

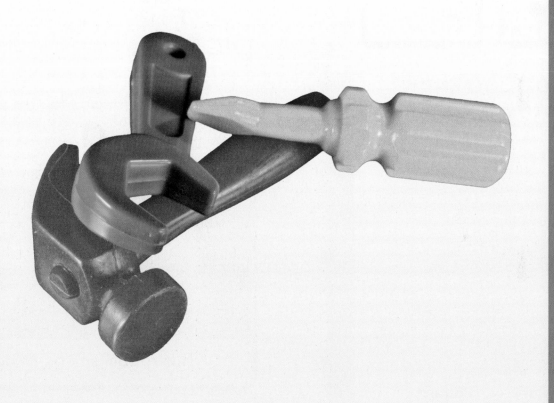

We like the 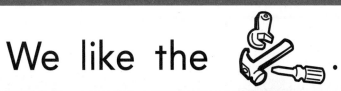.

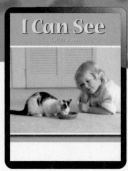

✓ **WORDS TO KNOW**
High-Frequency Words

a

Vocabulary Reader

Context Cards

K.RI.1.1 ask and answer questions about key details; **K.RI.3.7** describe relationships between illustrations and the text; **K.RF.3.3.c** read common high-frequency words by sight

Words to Know

Read Together

▸ Read the word.

▸ Talk about the picture.

a

This rabbit sits on a log.

Your Turn

Talk About It!

Why do different animals move in different ways? Talk about it with a friend.

Cc

by David Ashford

illustrated by John Segal

Cc

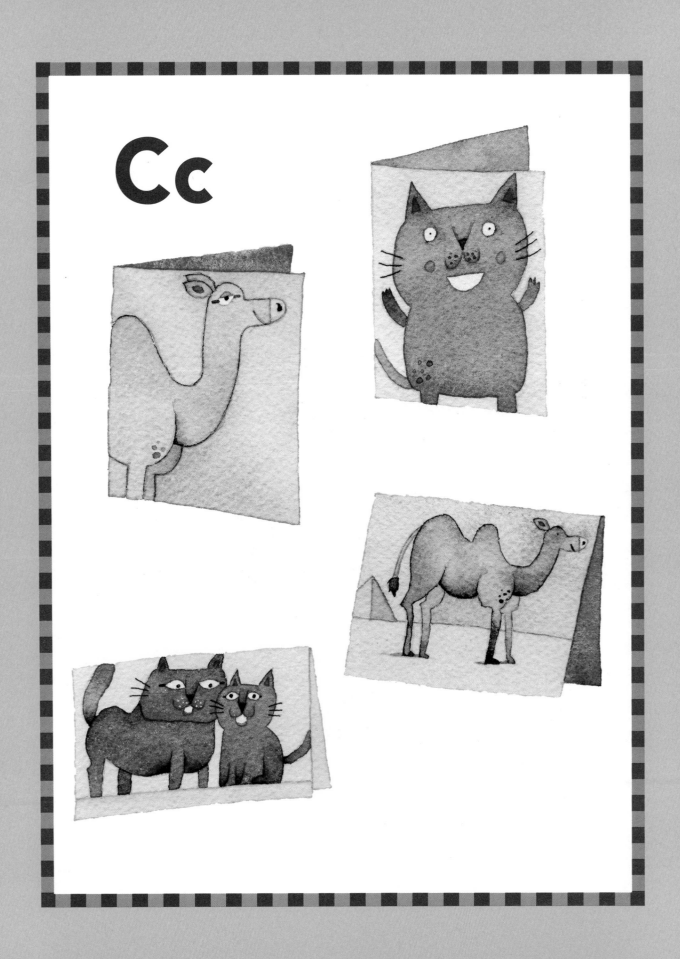

Cc

I Can See

by Laticia Craven

I see a .

Cc

I see a .

Cc

I see a .

Cc

I see a  .

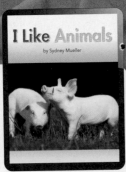

☑ **WORDS TO KNOW**
High-Frequency Words

to

Vocabulary Reader

Context Cards

K.RI.3.7 describe the relationship between illustrations and the text; **K.RF.3.3.c** read common high-frequency words by sight; **K.SL.1.2** confirm understanding of a text read aloud or information presented orally or through other media by asking/answering questions and requesting clarification

Words to Know

Read Together

▸ Read the word.

▸ Talk about the picture.

to

We like **to** ride our bikes!

Your Turn

Talk About It!

Why do people use wheels?
Talk with a partner.

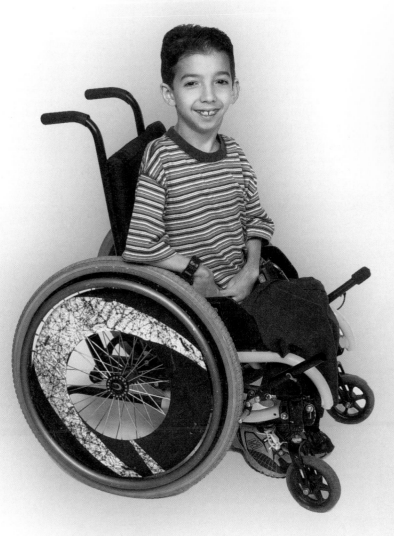

Pp

by Diondra Thomas
illustrated by Kristin Sorra

Pp

I Like Animals

by Sydney Mueller

I like to see 🐖🐖.

Pp

I like to see .

Pp

I like to see 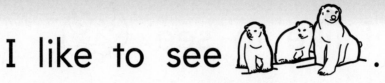 .

Pp

I like to see 🦜🦜.

Mmmm, Good!
by Angela Ferie
illustrated Ana Ochoa

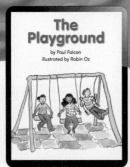

The Playground
by Paul Falcon
illustrated by Robin Oz

✓ **WORDS TO KNOW**
High-Frequency Words

see

we

Vocabulary
Reader

Context
Cards

K.RL.1.1 ask and answer questions about key details; **K.RL.1.3** identify characters, settings, and major events; **K.RF.3.3.c** read common high-frequency words by sight

98

Words to Know

Read Together

▸ You learned these words. Use each one in a sentence.

see

What can you **see** in the city?

we

Our cat purrs when **we** pet her.

Your Turn

Talk About It!

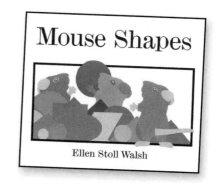

What can we create with shapes? Talk with a partner.

Mmmm, Good!

by Angela Ferie
illustrated Ana Ochoa

I see .

I like .

We like  .

We like to see .

The Playground

by Paul Falcon

illustrated by Robin Oz

I like the  .

I like to  .

We see the .

We like the 🎆.

Come and See Me
by Greg Kent

Pam and Me
by Louise Andreas
illustrated by Judith Lanfredi

✓ WORDS TO KNOW
High-Frequency Words

come

me

Vocabulary
Reader

Context
Cards

Fun in July
by Zachary Lambert

The rain will come down in spring.

K.RI.1.1 ask and answer questions about key details; **K.RI.4.10** engage in group reading activities with purpose and understanding; **K.RF.3.3.c** read common high-frequency words by sight

Go
Digital

Words
to Know

Read
Together

▸ Read the words.

▸ Talk about the pictures.

come

The rain will come down in spring.

me

This hat is for me.

108

Your Turn

Talk About It!

How does the weather change in different months and seasons? Talk to a friend about it.

JUMP
INTO JANUARY
A Journey Around the Year
Stella Blackstone
Maria Carluccio

Come and See Me

by Greg Kent

Pat Cat, Pat Cat!
Pat, Pat, Pat!

Come to me, Pat Cat!
Pat Cat sat.

Sam Cat, Sam Cat!
Sam, Sam, Sam!

Come to me, Sam Cat!
Sam Cat sat.

Pam and Me

by Louise Andreas

illustrated by Judith Lanfredi

Pam, Pam, Pam, Pam!

Pam, Pam, Pam.
Come to me, Pam.

I sat. Pam Cat sat.

I pat Pam.
Pat, pat, pat.

Lesson 12

I Can Nap
by Christopher Lawrence

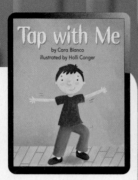
Tap with Me
by Cara Bianco
illustrated by Holli Conger

✓ **WORDS TO KNOW**
High-Frequency Words

with
my

Vocabulary Reader

Animals in the Snow

Context Cards

K.RL.1.1 ask and answer questions about key details; K.RF.3.3.c read common high-frequency words by sight

Go Digital

118

Words to Know

Read Together

‣ Read the words.

‣ Talk about the pictures.

with

1

The trees are covered with snow.

my

2

The snowman wears my scarf.

Your Turn

Talk About It!

snow

Manya Stojic

What do animals do when the weather changes? Talk to a partner about it.

I Can Nap

by Christopher Lawrence

 can nap.

Nap, nap, nap, nap.

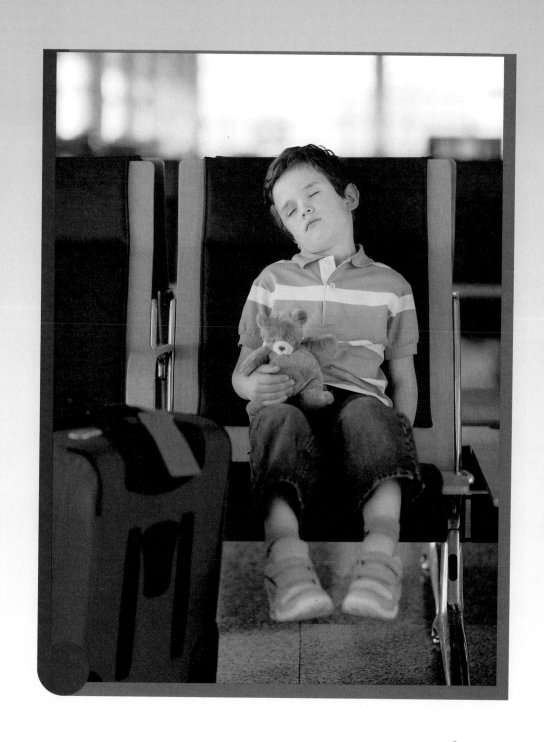

I can nap with my .
Nap, nap, nap, nap.

 can nap.

Nap, nap, nap, nap.

I can nap with my .
Nap, nap, nap, nap.

123

Tap with Me

by Cara Blanco

illustrated by Holli Conger

I can tap.

I tap, tap, tap.

I can nap with my .
Nap, nap, nap, nap.

Tap with Me

by Cara Blanco

illustrated by Holli Conger

I can tap.
I tap, tap, tap.

I can tap. Nan can tap.
Nan can tap, tap, tap.

I can tap with Nan.
Tap, tap, tap.

I am Tap Man!
Tap, tap, tap! Tap Man!

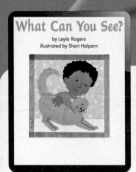

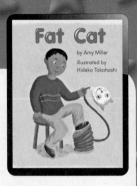

✓ **WORDS TO KNOW**
High-Frequency Words

you

what

Vocabulary Reader

Context Cards

K.RI.1.1 ask and answer questions about key details; **K.RF.3.3.c** read common high-frequency words by sight; **K.SL.1.1.a** follow rules for discussions

Words to Know

Read Together

▸ Read the words.

▸ Talk about the pictures.

you

Do you see the butterfly?

what

What colors do you see?

Your Turn

Talk About It!

How do animals use their body parts? Talk to a partner about it.

What Can You See?

by Leyla Rogers

illustrated by Shari Halpern

Cam can see a tan cat.

A tan, tan, tan cat!

Cam can see a fat tan cat.

Fan can see Nat.

Can Nat see Fan?

Nat can! Nat can!

Pam can see Sam nap.
Nap, nap, nap, Sam!

Can Mac see you?

Fat Cat

by Amy Miller

illustrated by

Hideko Takahashi

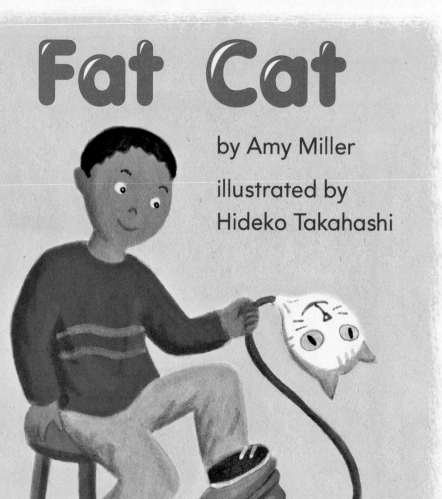

Can you see Sam?

Sam can tap, tap, tap.

Tap, Sam, tap.
Tap, tap, tap, Sam.

Tap, Sam!
Tap. Tap. Tap.

Can you see the fat cat?
What a fat, fat, fat cat!

14

What Now?
by Suzanne Gerardi

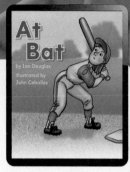
At Bat
by Ian Douglas
illustrated by
John Ceballos

 WORDS TO KNOW
High-Frequency Words

are

now

Vocabulary Reader

Context Cards

How Many Ducks?

K.RF.3.3.c read common high-frequency words by sight; **K.SL.1.2** confirm understanding of a text read aloud or information presented orally or through other media by asking/answering questions and requesting clarification

 Go Digital

138

Words to Know

▸ Read the words.

▸ Talk about the pictures.

are

The turtles **are** swimming.

now

The turtle is sleeping **now**.

Your Turn

Talk About It!

What animals can you find near a pond? Talk to a partner about it.

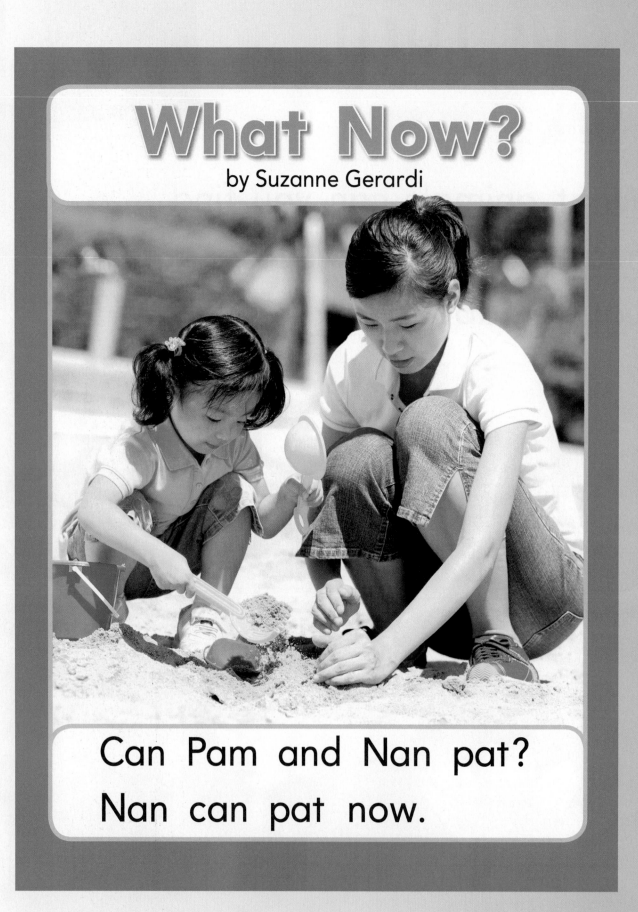

What Now?
by Suzanne Gerardi

Can Pam and Nan pat?
Nan can pat now.

Can Nat tap? Nat can!
Nat can tap now.

Sam and Bab are at bat.
Bat, Sam, bat!

Now we can nap, nap, nap.

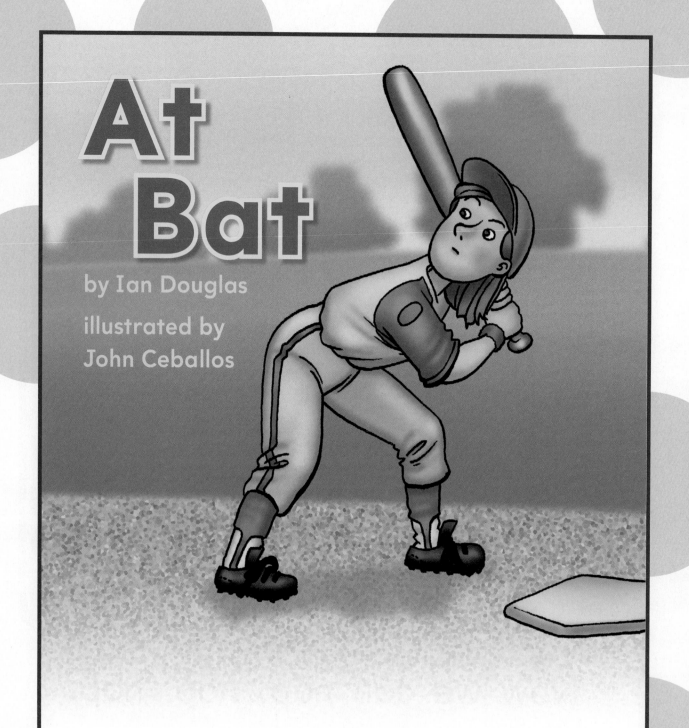

At Bat

by Ian Douglas

illustrated by
John Ceballos

See Bab at bat.
Bab can bat, bat, bat.

Bat now, Bab!
Bam!

See Pat.
Pat! Pat! Pat!

Pat! Pat! Pat! Pat!
We are , Pat!

Pam Cat
by Nina Dimopolous
illustrated by Bari Weissmann

Come with Me
by Roger DiPaulo
illustrated by Fahimeh Amiri

☑ **WORDS TO KNOW**
High-Frequency Words

come

me

Vocabulary Reader

Context Cards

In the Sky
by Daniel Morgan

HOUGHTON MIFFLIN

The rain will come down in spring.

K.RI.1.1 ask and answer questions about key details; **K.RI.1.2** identify the main topic and retell key details; **K.RF.3.3.c** read common high-frequency words by sight

Go Digital

Words to Know

Read Together

▸ You learned these words. Use each one in a sentence.

come

The rain will come down in spring.

me

This hat is for me.

Your Turn

Talk About It!

What can we see in the sky? Talk to a friend about it.

Pam Cat

by Nina Dimopolous

illustrated by Bari Weissmann

Mac sat and sat.

Pam Cat sat.
Mac can pat Pam Cat.

Pam Cat sat, sat, sat.
Mac can fan Pam Cat.

Pam, Pam, Pam!
Come to me, Pam Cat.

Come with Me

by Roger DiPaulo

illustrated by Fahimeh Amiri

Nat sat and sat.
Nat sat, sat, sat.

Come with me, Bab!
Bab! Bab! Bab!

Nat sat. Bab sat.
Nat can see Nan.
Bab can see Nan.

Nat sat. Bab sat. Nan sat.

Photo Credits

Placement Key: (r) right, (l) left, (c) center, (t) top, (b) bottom, (bg) background

---

3 (tl) Stephen Oliver/Alamy; (cl) Goodshot/Corbis; (b) Creatas/Jupiterimages/Getty Images; 4 (tl) Artville; (cl) © Liane Cary/AGE Fotostock; (b) ©Corbis; 5 (tl) Picture Partners/Alamy; (cl) Arco Images/Alamy; 6 (tl) William Manning/Corbis; (cl) Corbis RF/Alamy; 7 (t) © Geostock/Getty; (cl) Jupiterimages/BananaStock/Alamy; 8 (c) Big Cheese/SuperStock; 9 (tr) © Tom & Dee Ann McCarthy/Corbis; (b) Comstock/Getty Images; 18 (c) Brand X Pictures/Superstock; 19 (bl) © Prod. NumÃrik/Fotolia; (br) Comstock/Getty Images; 28 (c) Rubberball/Superstock; 29 (b) © Houghton Mifflin Harcourt/Houghton Mifflin Harcourt; 38 (tl) Stephen Oliver/Alamy; (c) Image Source/SuperStock; 39 (c) Alamy; (b) Digital Vision/Getty Images; 44 Stephen Oliver/Alamy; 45 Scott Camazine/Alamy; 46 ImageState/Alamy; 47 (inset) © ImageState/Alamy; Larry Williams/Corbis; 48 (tl) © Goodshoot/Corbis; Brand X Pictures/Superstock; (t) Big Cheese/SuperStock; 49 (b) Creatas/Jupiterimages/Getty Images; 54 © Goodshoot/Corbis; 55 © Craige Bevil/Alamy; 56 © Don Hammond/Design Pics/Corbis; 57 FoodCollection/AGE Fotostock; 58 (tl) Artville; (c) Joe Sohm/Pan America/Jupiterimages; 59 (bl) William Burlingham; (br) © Houghton Mifflin Harcourt/Houghton Mifflin Harcourt; 64 Artville; 65 PhotoDisc; 66 Jupiterimages/Comstock Images/Alamy; 67 Westend61/Alamy; 68 (tl) Liane Cary/Age Fotostock; (c) Reed Kaestner/Corbis; 69 (b) © Corbis; 74 Liane Cary/Age Fotostock; 75 George Doyle/Stockbyte/Getty Images; 76 C Squared Studios; 77 Nigel Hicks/Alamy; 78 (tl) © Picture Partners/Alamy; (c) Neo Vision/Getty Images; 79 (bl) © Kim Steele/Photodisc Green/Getty Images; (bc) JupiterImages/Polka Dot/Alamy; (br) Comstock/Getty Images; 84 © Picture Partners/Alamy; 85 Blend Images/Alamy; 86 © Tom Galliher/Corbis; 87 Picture Partners/Alamy; 88 (tl) Arco Images/Alamy; (c) PhotoDisc/Getty Images; 89 (bl) HRW Photo; (br) Creatas/Jupiterimages/Getty Images; 94 Arco Images/Alamy; 95 Corbis Super RF/Alamy; 96 © John Pitcher/AGE Fotostock; 97 © imagebroker/Alamy; 98 (t) Joe Sohm/Pan America/Jupiterimages; (b) Reed Kaestner/Corbis; 99 © Houghton Mifflin Harcourt; 108 (tl) © William Manning/Corbis; (t) © Corbis Premium RF/Almay; (b) Image Source/Superstock; 109 (b) © Getty Images; 110 William Manning/Corbis; 111 Brand X Pictures; 112 Getty Images; 113 Peter Arnold, Inc./Alamy; 118 (tl) Corbis RF/Alamy; (t) Joseph De sciose/Nonstock/Jupiterimages; (b) Thinkstock Images/Jupiterimages; 119 (b) Ilene MacDonald/Almay Images; 120 Corbis RF/Alamy; 121 Corbis; 122 © Wildseedmedia.com/Wildlife/Alamy; 123 © Jupiterimages/Polka Dot/Alamy; 128 (t) Image Source/Superstock; (b) Lee Cannon/OnAsia.com/Jupiterimages; 129 Brand X Pictures/Getty Images; 138 (tl) Jupiterimages/Creatas/Alamy; (t) Mathew Oldfield, Scubazoo/SPL/Photo Researchers, Inc.; (b) © Trevor Booth Photography/Alamy Images; 139 (bl) © Steve Hamblin/Alamy; (bc) © Geostock/Getty; (br) © Sylwia Domaradzka/Alamy; 140 Jupiterimages/Creatas/Alamy; 141 © Elvele Images/Alamy; 142 Jupiterimages/Polka Dot/Alamy; 143 © Image Source Black/Alamy; 148 (t) Ken McGraw/Index Stock Imagery/Jupiterimages; (b) Image Source/Superstock; 149 (tr) © BananaStock/SuperStock; (b) Digital Vision/Getty Images.